Electa Quinney

Badger Biographies

Other Badger Biographies

Electa Quinney

Stockbridge Teacher

KARYN SAEMANN

WISCONSIN HISTORICAL SOCIETY PRESS

Published by the Wisconsin Historical Society Press
Publishers since 1855

wisconsin**history**.org

Photographs identified with WHi are from the Society's collections; address requests to reproduce these photos to the Visual Materials Archivist at the Wisconsin Historical Society, 816 State Street, Madison, WI 53706.

Front cover: Photograph courtesy of the National Museum of the American Indian
Back cover: WHi Image ID 41576

Printed in Wisconsin, USA
Cover and interior design by Jill Bremigan
Interior page composition by Biner Design

18 17 16 15 14   1 2 3 4 5

Library of Congress Cataloging-in-Publication Data

Saemann, Karyn.
  Electa Quinney : Stockbridge teacher / Karyn Saemann.
     p. cm. — (Badger biographies)
  Includes bibliographical references and index.
  ISBN 978-0-87020-641-2 (pbk.) — ISBN 978-0-87020-642-9 (ebook) 1. Quinney, Electa, 1807-1882. 2. Stockbridge Indians—Wisconsin—Biography. 3. Indian women teachers—Wisconsin—Biography. I. Title.
  E99.S8.Q85S34 2014
  305.897'3449092—dc23
  [B]
                                    2013036971

∞ The paper used in this publication meets the minimum requirements of the American National Standard for Information Sciences—Permanence of Paper for Printed Library Materials, ANSI Z39.48-1992.

Publication of this book was made possible in part
by a grant from the D.C. Everest fellowship fund.

Contents

1

Meet Electa Quinney

In 1828, a smart young woman named Electa Quinney did something very important in Wisconsin history. She became the state's first public schoolteacher.

At that time, there were only a few towns in Wisconsin. Rough dirt roads and winding rivers carried travelers through thick forests and swamps. In towns in the woods, there were just a handful of schools. Most of the teachers were men.

Electa Quinney was different. She was a young woman who was a schoolteacher. What made her even more different was that she was a Stockbridge Indian.

Many Wisconsin Indians in 1828 had a **culture** similar to how they had lived for thousands of years. They gathered plants for medicine, dressed in animal skins, and lived in **wigwams**.

culture: the way of life, ideas, and traditions of a group of people   **wigwam**: a home made of cattail mats or tree bark attached to a framework of small branches

They fished and hunted for food from Wisconsin's forests and streams. Many of them spoke only their native language and didn't go to school. **Missionaries** had taught many of them about Christianity, but most Wisconsin Indians kept the religion that they had grown up with.

WHI IMAGE ID 1000I

Wigwams

missionaries (**mish** uh nair ee): someone who travels to spread a religion and to do good work

The Stockbridge Indians were different. They moved to Wisconsin from New York in the 1820s. When they arrived, the Stockbridge built homes made of logs. They grew crops and raised animals on farms. Women spun wool, knitted, and sewed clothes from cloth. Many of them spoke English and went to church.

Like many other Stockbridge Indians, Electa went to **boarding schools** when she was young. She learned to speak and write English well. This made her an excellent schoolteacher.

There are many things we don't know about Electa. We don't know exactly when or where she was born, though it was somewhere in the state of New York. We don't know what she looked like when she was young. We have only one photo of Electa. It was taken in the 1860s, around the time when she became a grandmother. And there are a few times in Electa's life when we're not sure where she was living or what she was doing. She left behind no diary or other written memories.

boarding school: a school at which students live during the school year

3

Understanding Electa's life is like working on a jigsaw puzzle.

Understanding Electa's life is like working on a jigsaw puzzle. We need to fit together many little pieces from many different places. Some of the puzzle pieces of Electa's story are missing, so we have an incomplete picture of her life.

Some of what we know about Electa is found in letters written by her friends and family. Other people who knew Electa wrote down thoughts and memories about her.

4

We also have a few words she said to a judge, some **legal** papers she signed, and a letter she wrote for older Stockbridge Indians who could not write in English.

We are certain about some things. We know that soon after she arrived in Wisconsin, Electa taught at a school in an Indian village called Statesburg. Electa's school was made of logs, and it was surrounded by thick woods. Her students studied many of the same subjects children learn about today, such as math, spelling, and geography.

We know that Electa was a good teacher. She had many friends and she loved to read. Visitors to her home said that it was filled with books and that they enjoyed talking to her.

Sometimes Electa had to make difficult choices. Once, she made a tough decision to move to **Indian Territory**, near what would later become the state of Oklahoma. A few years after that, Electa said good-bye to her friends there and moved back to Wisconsin.

legal: having to do with laws   **Indian Territory**: a large area of the United States set aside in 1834 where only Indians could live

5

What's the toughest choice you've ever had to make? One of Electa's most difficult decisions came near the end of her life. The Stockbridge Indians and their friends, the Munsee Indians, had to decide whether to become US **citizens**. If they became citizens, Stockbridge and Munsee Indians would no longer be members of their own tribe. What did Electa choose? The answer tells us a lot about Electa and a lot about the Stockbridge Indians.

citizen: someone who is an official member of a country or state and has a right to live there

2

New York Childhood

Electa was born around 1807 in the state of New York. She was probably born in New Stockbridge, an Indian village in the middle of the state. Many lakes and streams and good farmland surrounded the village. When the Stockbridge Indians chose their new home in Wisconsin in the 1820s, they picked a place that reminded them of New Stockbridge.

By the time Electa was born, most Stockbridge Indians lived differently than their **ancestors** had in the past. They had **assimilated** many parts of European culture. Missionaries who visited the tribe in New Stockbridge in 1796 said men were raising sheep and crops on farms. Stockbridge women were spinning wool to sell. The tribe had a sawmill and a school, and they were planning to build a blacksmith shop.

ancestor: a family member from long ago   **assimilated**: took in and made as one's own

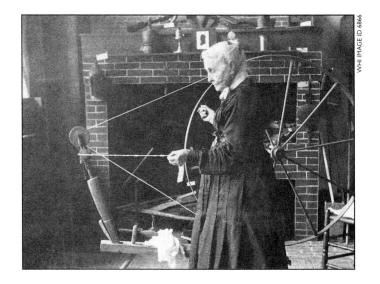

In the 1700s, Stockbridge Indian women learned to sew, knit, and spin yarn, like the woman shown here.

WHI IMAGE ID 6866

"The **sachem** Hendrick Apaumut has a good field of wheat, Indian corn, potatoes and grass, and we had the pleasure of meeting him in the road driving his ox team," the missionaries wrote.

"Almost every family has sowed wheat this fall," wrote another visitor in 1796.

Many Stockbridge were also going to church. And their native language, **Mohican**, was being replaced by English. One **historian** wrote in 1809, "Many of these Indians could read English, and . . . some few could write."

sachem (**sa** chum): tribal leader   **Mohican**: moh **hee** kuhn   **historian**: a person who studies and writes about the past

Who Are the Stockbridge Indians?

The Stockbridge are Mohican Indians. The name *Mohican* comes from the **Muhheakantuck**, a river that flows through eastern New York. The Mohicans lived near the Muhheakantuck River for about 2,000 years. They call themselves *Muh-he-ka-ne-ok*, which means "people of the waters that are never still." The Muhheakantuck River is now known as the Hudson River, named for the explorer Henry Hudson. It is still one of the most important rivers in New York.

Beginning in 1730, the Mohican Indians moved many times. They moved to Massachusetts, where people started to call them the Stockbridge Indians. Then they moved to central New York, where Electa was probably born. Finally, they came to Wisconsin.

In Wisconsin, the Stockbridge lived on the Fox River and then on the eastern shore of Lake Winnebago. In 1856, the Stockbridge Indians and their friends, the Munsee Indians, moved to a new **reservation** near Shawano, Wisconsin. Today, the combined tribe is known as the Stockbridge-Munsee Band of Mohican Indians, and many of them still live on the reservation near Shawano.

A Mohican sachem, Etowaukaum, in 1710

Muhheakantuck: muh **hee** kahn tuck   **reservation**: government land reserved or set aside for Indian nations to live on

Electa belonged to a well-known Stockbridge family. "This family seems to have been more **distinguished** during the whole course of their history as Stockbridge Indians, than any other," one historian wrote.

We can't say for sure who Electa's father was. Records from the time are not very clear. Electa's brother John said that his father was Joseph Quinney, and he was probably Electa's father, too. He was a Stockbridge sachem.

Joseph Quinney's father, John Quan-au-kaunt, was also an important tribal member. John Quan-au-kaunt could speak and read English at a time when most people in his tribe only spoke Mohican. He was famous for translating a **catechism** from English into Mohican so the Stockbridge Indians could read it. He worked as a schoolteacher.

Electa's mother, Margaret Quinney, came from an important family, too. Her father was David Nau-nau-neek-nuk, and he was a Stockbridge Indian sachem. He was a fierce warrior who fought on the side of the American Colonies in the Revolutionary War.

distinguished (dis **ting** guishd): well known and respected   **catechism** (**kat** uh kiz uhm): a manual that teaches religious beliefs

Margaret Quinney's grandfather was also named David Nau-nau-neek-nuk. He was a warrior, a Stockbridge tribal leader, and "the owner of 60 horses." He was one of the first Mohican Indians **baptized** by Christian missionaries. John Sergeant, a missionary to the Mohican Indians, once called him a man "of very good **temper** and good sense."

Two of Electa's brothers, John and Austin, grew up to be tribal leaders.

Spirit Names

John *Quan-au-kaunt*, David *Nau-nau-neek-nuk*—these are traditional Indian names. The Stockbridge-Munsee Indians call them spirit names. They believe that a child's spirit name is chosen for them before they are born. It has special meaning for their life ahead.

But what do these names mean? We're not always sure. The spirit names of Stockbridge Indians from long ago are in Mohican, and today there are no Mohican **native speakers**. Figuring out what Mohican words mean is often hard work.

---

baptized (bap tɪzd): sprinkled with or dunked in water as a sign of becoming a Christian   **temper**: a person's usual attitude or mood   **native speaker**: a person who learns a language as a baby

11

Electa had a spirit name. She signed legal papers as "Electa W. Quinney." The "W" stands for Wuh-weh-wee-nee-meew. What does it mean in Mohican? Jeremy Mohawk is a member of the Stockbridge-Munsee tribe who studies the Munsee and Mohican languages. He believes Electa's name has something to do with "knowing." That certainly fits Electa the schoolteacher.

Electa's last name, Quinney, also means something interesting. Quinney is short for Quan-au-kaunt, the spirit name of Electa's grandfather. In Mohican, Quan-au-kaunt means "appearing to be tall." Someone once wrote that Electa was tall, so that fits her, too.

Stockbridge-Munsee Indians learn their spirit name in a special **ceremony** after they are born. According to them, a person's spirit, which can't be seen and is separate from their body, secretly tells the name to an older relative, such as an aunt or an uncle. This happens before the baby is born. The name is then announced at the ceremony.

Electa's brother John's spirit name was Waun-nau-con. In Mohican, this means "wooden dinner plate." That sounds funny, but it must have had an important meaning that we don't understand today. Electa's brother Austin's spirit name was Ikutauam, which means "both sides of the river."

Once, it was common for Stockbridge and Munsee Indians to know their spirit name. But in the 1900s, most parents stopped

ceremony (**ser** uh moh nee): a formal event to mark an important occasion

12

holding ceremonies for their babies. Around the same time, the last Mohican native speakers died. For many years, no one spoke Mohican and very few Stockbridge or Munsee Indians knew their spirit names.

But a few native speakers remained among the Munsee. Because the Munsee and Mohican languages are very similar, it is possible to speak in Mohican if you first learn Munsee. Now these Munsee Indians are helping younger Munsee and the Stockbridge relearn their languages. At the same time, members of the Stockbridge-Munsee tribe are studying the spirit names of their ancestors, like Electa, to figure out what they mean. And parents are again giving new babies spirit names in special ceremonies.

WHI IMAGE ID 1923

Electa's brother, Austin Ikutauam Quinney. The spirit name Ikutauam means "both sides of the river."

13

WHI IMAGE ID 74339

A dormitory

When she was a girl, Electa left home to go to boarding school. Both Indian and white students lived together at the school. They did chores, played, and ate together. They slept together in a **dormitory**. Indian students like Electa practiced reading and writing English and made new friends. They didn't go home very often. Sometimes an entire school year or longer passed between visits home to their families.

dormitory: a large room with many beds for sleeping

14

The first boarding school Electa went to was in Clinton, New York. It was called the Clinton **Female Seminary**. It was a well-known school. Girls from some of the most important families in New York and Canada, both Indian and white, went there. The school was run by a teacher named Nancy Royce. Nancy did not open her school until 1814. That means Electa was at least 7 years old before she went to school there.

At the Clinton Female Seminary, girls studied many subjects. Like students today, they learned about grammar, math, geography, history, reading, and writing. The girls also worked on their penmanship and **orthography**. They even studied some subjects children rarely learn about today, such as map drawing, astronomy, needlework, and **stenography**. They worked hard. Do *you* know what year the Roman Empire began? This was a question in a history textbook used by Clinton Female Seminary students in the 1820s.

female seminary: a school where girls were taught to be proper ladies   **orthography** (or **thog** ruh fee): spelling   **stenography** (stuh **nog** ruh fee): note taking

15

Tuition was 5 dollars. Lessons in advanced subjects, such as chemistry, algebra, drawing, painting, French, or music, cost extra. Meals and a bedroom cost $1.50 a week. Laundry was 25 cents for a dozen pieces of clothing. Students had to bring their own candles, candlesticks, **snuffers**, and towels.

Nancy Royce took good care of her students. She made sure they exercised, used good manners, and kept their clothes and bodies looking nice. "The Young Ladies who

At boarding school, Electa learned to do needlework like these girls.

WHI IMAGE ID 65025

tuition: money paid to take classes   **snuffer**: a tool used for putting out candles

The building that held the Clinton Female Seminary still stands. This is where Electa went to school.

board in the Seminary will be considered as members of the family," Royce wrote. She also taught students about the Christian religion.

After this, Electa went to a boarding school on Long Island, New York. It was a **Quaker** school. Electa probably left home with 6 other girls in 1818. She went to the Quaker school for 4 years, from when she was 11 to when she was 15.

Quaker: a Christian group founded in the 1600s, also called the Religious Society of Friends

Electa was not the first Stockbridge Indian to attend a Quaker boarding school. The Quakers had many boarding schools, and Stockbridge children had been going to them for many years.

The first Stockbridge children to study with Quakers left home in 1797. That year, 6 girls went to live with Quaker families in Pennsylvania. There they learned "spinning, weaving, how to make butter and other such things that are useful on a farm." They also learned to read and write English. Stockbridge tribal leaders, including Joseph Quinney, wrote "we **heartily** thank you" in a letter to the Quakers after the girls returned in 1801. In 1810, Electa's brother John went to a Quaker school for boys in New York.

One of the Stockbridge girls who left for boarding school in 1818 wanted to be a weaver. Another wanted to be a teacher. Was this future teacher Electa? Probably. We know nothing else about this time in Electa's life, only that many years later she said the Quakers were kind to her.

heartily: deeply and with all your heart

When she was done going to school, Electa became a teacher in New York. There was "a capable young woman" teaching school in New Stockbridge in 1822. She had 35 students. This was likely Electa.

Electa taught in New York for 6 years. Then, in 1828, when she was about 21 years old, her life changed forever. Electa left New York and moved to Wisconsin.

3
The Stockbridge Indians

Why did Electa and other Stockbridge Indians move to Wisconsin? To answer this question, it's helpful to understand the history of the tribe.

For more than 2,000 years, the Stockbridge lived along the Muhheakantuck River in New York. At that time, they were known as the Mohican Indians. They made maple syrup, hunted, fished, and grew just enough food to feed their families. They got along well with other Indian tribes.

In 1609, the world changed for the Mohicans. They met the explorer Henry Hudson along the Muhheakantuck River. He was the first white person they had ever met. It was a meeting that the Mohicans had long expected.

"Wise men **foretold** the coming of a strange race, from the sunrise, as numerous as the leaves upon the trees," Electa's

foretold: said ahead of time that some event would happen

WHI IMAGE ID 5224

Making maple syrup

brother John said in a speech in Reidsville, New York, in 1854. John and other Stockbridge Indians believed this **prophecy** came true when Europeans arrived in North America.

"Their number was small, but their canoes were big," John said.

prophecy (**prof** uh see): a statement or warning that something will happen in the future

Henry Hudson's ship on the Muhheakantuck River

LIBRARY OF CONGRESS, PRINTS AND PHOTOGRAPHS DIVISION, LC-USZ62-61745

In 1609, when they met Henry Hudson, the Mohican Indians wore belts made of **wampum**. These belts were traded among Indians at marriages or other special occasions. When white people came, the Mohicans traded wampum with them for things like blankets, iron tools, and guns. The Mohicans also took part in the **fur trade** with the new arrivals.

But later in the 1600s, lots of new white **settlers** began arriving in eastern New York. Life got harder for the Mohicans.

wampum: beads made from polished and carved shells and strung together to make belts, collars, and necklaces   **fur trade**: the exchange of goods such as metal knives and guns for animal pelts   **settlers**: people who make their home in a new country or area

White settlers brought with them terrible diseases such as smallpox, tuberculosis, and measles. Native people had never had these diseases before, and many Mohican Indians died from them. White settlers also sold alcohol to Indians, which upset tribal leaders. And they cut down forests in New York to make room for homes and farms.

The Mohicans became surrounded by settlers. They were no longer free to hunt and fish wherever they pleased. Settlers farmed the land and put up fences. By the 1700s, many animals that the Mohicans depended on for food, clothing, and trade began to disappear from New York's forests. This was due to hunting by settlers and Indians and loss of the animals' **habitats** as new towns and farms were built.

For many years, the Mohicans had especially relied on beaver fur to trade. The fur was turned into beautiful coats and hats. As beavers became harder to find, and as more white settlers crowded into eastern New York, the Mohicans had to make a big decision.

habitat: the place or environment where a plant or animal naturally or normally lives and grows

23

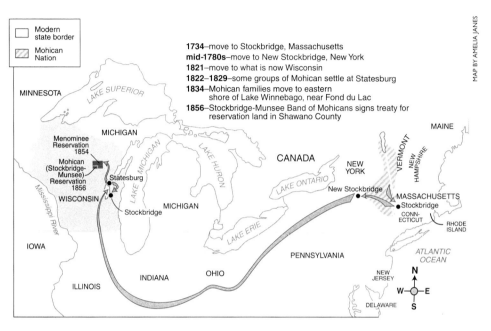

Journey of the Mohican Nation, Stockbridge-Munsee Band

In 1730, the Mohicans decided to move away from New York. Their new home was in the mountains in **remote** western Massachusetts, amid quiet lakes and rivers. There they could hunt and fish on their own.

In Massachusetts, the Mohicans first lived in a few scattered villages along the **Housatonic** River. The few white

remote: far away from other people or cities   **Housatonic**: haw suh **ton** ik

people who lived nearby called them the Housatonic Indians, after the river, or simply River Indians.

But the Mohicans were not alone for very long. In 1734, a missionary named John Sergeant visited them. He wanted to live with them and teach them about the Christian religion. The Mohicans had another big decision to make. Should they let John Sergeant teach them?

Many Mohicans liked that John was well educated and that he had gone to college. Others were interested in becoming Christians.

John Sergeant promised to start a school for Mohican children. He would teach them to be Christians and to speak, read, and write in English. Many Mohican parents liked that idea. Giving up some native ways might be worth it if their children could read and write in English.

But not all Mohicans were sure that letting John live with them was a good idea. They worried that if they learned to live more like white people, their Mohican culture would be lost.

John Sergeant came to live with the Stockbridge Indians in 1734.

Mohican leaders came together and talked for 4 days. In the end, they decided to let John Sergeant come live with them. Soon, many Stockbridge Indians became Christians, and their children began going to school and learning English.

In 1737, the **colonial** government of Massachusetts created a new Indian town called Stockbridge. It was along the Housatonic River, near where the Mohicans lived. Colonial leaders invited all Mohicans to live in this town together.

colonial (kuh **loh** nee uhl): of or about a colony

They said having all of the Mohicans living together, rather than in scattered villages, would make the work of missionaries and schoolteachers easier. There could be one church and one school building for everyone.

But the colonial leaders had another reason to suggest this. Many white settlers were afraid of Indians. Having the Mohicans all live in one place made white settlers feel safer. They would be less likely to run into them.

IMAGE COURTESY OF BLOOMSBURG UNIVERSITY

The Mohicans agreed to live in the town of Stockbridge. Soon, people started calling them the Stockbridge Indians.

The Stockbridge lived in Massachusetts for 55 years. During that time, some Stockbridge Indians fought on the side of the American Colonies in the Revolutionary War.

A Stockbridge Indian who fought on the side of the American Colonies in the Revolutionary War

27

In the war, which lasted from 1775 to 1783, the American Colonies won their **independence** from Great Britain. The United States of America was born.

But after the war, as had happened in New York, life in Massachusetts got harder for the Stockbridge.

When they returned from fighting, some Stockbridge Indian soldiers found white settlers living on their land. And all around them, new settlers were building homes and farms. Massachusetts was getting crowded.

In 1785, the Oneida Indians in New York invited the Stockbridge to live near them. The Oneidas gave the Stockbridge a few **acres** of land to live on. They called their new home New Stockbridge.

For a few years the Stockbridge were happy. But once again, their happiness didn't last. In 1785, only 2 white families lived nearby. By 1796, New Stockbridge was entirely surrounded by the farms of white settlers.

independence: the right to live freely, without being ruled by another government   acre (**ay** kur): an area of land almost as large as a football field

Where did all these people come from? Many new **immigrants** were arriving in America. Ships full of people came to the United States every day. During the years 1780 to 1860, more than 5 million immigrants arrived in the United States. Most were from European countries such as Ireland and Germany. They came to the United States to escape **famine**, religious **persecution**, and **revolutions** in their own countries.

immigrant (**im** uh gruhnt): someone who leaves one country to permanently live in another country
famine: a serious and widespread lack of food   **persecution**: cruel and unfair treatment because of religion or beliefs   **revolution**: a sudden and violent overthrow of a government or ruler

The Erie Canal

The Erie **Canal** helped bring many immigrants to New York. It was built between 1817 and 1825. The canal stretched for 363 miles across New York, from the Hudson River at Albany to Lake Erie at Buffalo. It allowed boats to travel nonstop all the way from the Atlantic Ocean to the Great Lakes. This was much quicker and safer than traveling by land.

All along the Erie Canal, new towns sprang up. One section of the canal passed by **Utica**, New York, just a few miles north of New Stockbridge.

PAINTING BY JOHN WILLIAM HILL

The Erie Canal

canal: a waterway made by people   **Utica: yoo** ti kuh

Immigrants wanted to build their homes and farms on Indian land. Companies that made money buying and selling land and government leaders in New York agreed with the immigrants. They **pressured** Indian tribes to sell their land and to leave the state.

The Stockbridge agreed to move. The pressure on them was great. Had they refused to move, the US government could have forced them to go anyway.

In Wisconsin, the Menominee Indians said they had land that the Stockbridge, Oneida, and other Indians from New York could live on. In 1822, the Stockbridge accepted the Menominees' offer. They left New York for Wisconsin. A few Stockbridge Indians who had moved to Indiana in 1818 came to Wisconsin, too.

Some Stockbridge Indians were glad to leave New York. White people selling alcohol to Indians was still a problem. And white settlers often **trespassed** on tribal members' land.

pressured: demanded that someone make a decision   **trespassed**: illegally went onto someone else's property

One Stockbridge woman said she was eager to get away. She said that white people treated Indians like children who needed taking care of. "We want none of their care, we are quite capable of caring for . . . ourselves," she said.

In 1829, John Quinney, Electa's brother, helped bring the last members of the Stockbridge tribe to Wisconsin. They had a new home and a new life.

4

To Wisconsin

Electa arrived in Wisconsin on June 20, 1828. At the time, Wisconsin was not yet a state. It was part of **Michigan Territory**. Wisconsin wouldn't become its own state for another 20 years.

Wisconsin's forests were full of wild animals, such as wolves and bears. There were also other Indians. Four of the 7 Indian groups that live in Wisconsin today were already living in the area long before 1828.

WHI IMAGE ID 57369

There were many wolves in Wisconsin in 1828.

Michigan Territory: a large area of the northern United States, near the Great Lakes, that included the future states of Michigan, Wisconsin, Iowa, and Minnesota and parts of North and South Dakota

These were the Menominee, Ho-Chunk, Ojibwe, and Potawatomi. The other 3 Indian nations—the Stockbridge-Munsee, Brothertown, and Oneida—began arriving in the 1820s.

When Electa came to Wisconsin, there were only a few scattered towns. Madison and Milwaukee, 2 big cities today, did not exist yet. Wisconsin's first newspaper wasn't printed until 1833. The first bank didn't open until 1835. In 1828, most white people who lived in Wisconsin worked as lead miners, missionaries, fur traders, or lumberjacks. Some were soldiers at 3 United States military forts.

People mostly traveled by lake or by river. Roads were rare, and Wisconsin's first railroads weren't built until the 1850s. Travelers often used the Fox and Wisconsin Rivers to get from one place to another.

Statesburg, where Electa first lived, was along the Fox River between Green Bay and Lake Winnebago. It was near a spot on the river called the Grand **Kaukaulin**. Today, the

Kaukaulin: kah **kaw** lin

34

In the 1820s, travel in Wisconsin was usually by canoe on rivers and lakes.

Grand Kaukaulin is still a beautiful place. There are high **bluffs** along the river and many small islands. Ducks swim among the islands.

Grand comes from the French word for "big." And *Kaukaulin* comes from a Menominee Indian word that means "where the fish stop." This was once a popular fishing spot for the Menominee Indians.

bluff: a cliff or steep natural wall

In Wisconsin, Electa lived along the Fox River, at a place called the Grand Kaukaulin.

The Grand Kaukaulin has many rocky **rapids**. In Electa's time, it was a dangerous spot for travelers. The current is swift at the rapids, and the river quickly drops more than 40 feet in **elevation**.

Most travelers got out of the river at the rapids and **portaged** their canoes. This made the Grand Kaukaulin an important trading post. Travelers bought supplies there.

rapids: a place in a river where water flows very fast **elevation** (eh leh **vay** shun): the height of land
portaged: carried boats and supplies overland between 2 waterways or around a rough part such as a waterfall

Later, in the 1850s, **locks** and dams were built, making boat travel easier.

On August 1, 1828, a missionary named Jesse Miner mentioned Electa in a letter. Jesse said Electa arrived in Green Bay from New York on June 20. She had traveled to Wisconsin with him and some other Stockbridge Indians. They made their new home in Statesburg.

WHI IMAGE ID 91138

A lock at the Grand Kaukaulin

lock: a section of a canal that is closed off with gates. A ship can be raised or lowered in a lock by pumping water in or out.

That summer, Electa began teaching school in Statesburg. She taught subjects such as math and reading, and her students learned about the Christian religion.

"She is a person of good education," Jesse wrote. "She is very **faithful** to the children."

On October 5, 1828, Electa's name appeared on a list of people attending the church in Statesburg. The mission house, or church building, was made of logs. It was also Electa's school.

Electa's school wasn't the first one in Wisconsin. There were a few private schools in other places. But it was Wisconsin's very first public school, and Electa was Wisconsin's first public schoolteacher.

Public Schools and Private Schools

What's the difference between a public school and a private school? The main difference is in how teachers are paid. Everyone whose home is near a public school gives some money to pay the teachers. They do this even if they don't have children because they agree it is important to have a school.

faithful: loyal and caring

In Statesburg, Stockbridge tribal leaders paid Electa with money collected from members of the tribe. Today, money to pay public school teachers is collected through **taxes**.

Private schools are not paid for by everyone in a community. Usually, just the families of students pay the teacher. In 1830, a school in Mineral Point charged a tuition of $2.50 for younger children and $3.50 for older children.

The students at the first private school in Wisconsin were all from one family. This was in 1791. They were the children of a French fur trader in Green Bay. The fur trader paid a private teacher to instruct his children.

Some private schoolteachers before 1828 were paid by the US military. In 1817, the first school in Wisconsin for children of soldiers opened at Fort Crawford in Prairie du Chien. The teacher was an army sergeant.

Other private schoolteachers were paid by churches. In 1823, a missionary opened a private school near Green Bay. About 50 children went to this school. The church paid the teacher.

tax: money paid to a government

At first, only Indian children went to Electa's school. Then, in November 1828, Jesse Miner's children arrived with their mother from New York. They were the first white children at Electa's school. Many years later, Jesse's son, **Eliphalet**, said Electa was a good teacher. Eliphalet is the only student of Electa's whose memories were written down and saved.

Electa "was a better teacher than the average of teachers," Eliphalet said. He said her classroom was like "the best public schools of New England." In addition to math and reading, Electa taught Eliphalet spelling, public speaking, and geography. She began each day with a prayer.

Eliphalet also recalled that Electa was kind. At this time,

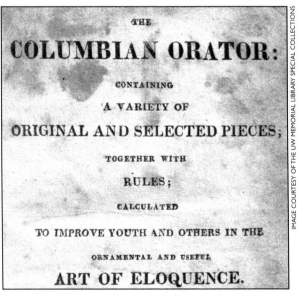

IMAGE COURTESY OF THE UW MEMORIAL LIBRARY SPECIAL COLLECTIONS

Eliphalet Miner said he used this textbook in Electa's classroom at Statesburg.

Eliphalet: i **lif** uh let

it was still considered okay for teachers to whip naughty children by hitting them with rope or a thin stick. "She rarely whipped," Eliphalet said.

Another teacher, Augustus Ambler, arrived in Statesburg in November 1828. He lived with Jesse's family and taught at the school for a few months. Electa took over again in 1829.

"I have taught their school 3 months," Augustus wrote in a letter in March 1829. "The Indians have agreed with Mr. [Miner] to pay me $24 per month for teaching the winter school. Electa Quinney, a **competent** native teacher, will probably take charge of the school this summer and be paid from public funds of the Indians."

In 1829, Electa helped some older Stockbridge Indian women write a letter to friends back East. Things were going well in Wisconsin, the letter said. "The people have much improved since leaving New York," Electa wrote.

competent (**kom** puh tuhnt): capable

41

A missionary named Cutting Marsh came to Statesburg in 1830. He agreed that things were going well for the Stockbridge in Wisconsin. He wrote that the Stockbridge Indians were going to church. Each family lived in their own house made of logs and had a farm with animals and a barn. "Their houses in winter are very comfortable," Marsh said.

Electa also had fun. She was young and not yet married. One person wrote that she was well liked and "moved in [the] best society at Fort Howard."

Fort Howard

Fort Howard was in Green Bay. Many young soldiers lived at the fort. They invited young people like Electa to dances.

What were dances like at Fort Howard? Marie Brevoort, whose father was an **Indian agent**, went to a dance at Fort Howard in July 1827. Marie said dinner was served early in the evening, followed by dancing until midnight to a military band. "The music was **enchanting**," Marie recalled.

Marie's dress that evening was light purple and had white lace. She wore long white gloves and red slippers. On her shoulders was a white lace shawl, and on her head she wore a large green **calash**.

IMAGE COURTESY OF THE COLLECTIONS OF OLD STURBRIDGE VILLAGE

A calash

Another young woman in the area was Elizabeth Baird. She was 14 years old and newly married when she came to Green Bay in 1824. Her husband, Henry Baird, was a lawyer. Many years later, he became mayor of Green Bay.

Indian agent: someone who worked for the US government and whose job was to communicate with Indian tribes   **enchanting**: delightful and charming   **calash**: a large, folding hood worn by women in the 1800s

43

Elizabeth said young people went on picnics and canoe trips up the Fox River. When there was not a dance at Fort Howard, they danced and ate supper at the homes of their friends. In the winter, they went on sleigh rides.

One family had 4 sons Elizabeth's age. They were all musicians, Elizabeth remembered. "Louis, the eldest, was our fiddler. Whenever we made up a sleigh-ride party we were always accompanied by Louis **Ducharme**."

A fiddle player

Ducharme: du **shahrm**

Louis was from a well-known family. The Ducharmes were some of the first French settlers in Green Bay. A few years after this, Electa's older sister Phebe married Louis Ducharme.

Perhaps on a sleigh ride, as Louis Ducharme played the fiddle, Electa met

Ebenezer Childs. In 1829, Ebenezer was the sheriff of Brown County. One story says that Ebenezer asked Electa to marry him. Electa told him no. She wanted to marry an Indian man.

We don't know if this really happened. But we do know some things about Ebenezer. Later in life, he recalled that he had been a "stubborn, hot-headed young man." He got into trouble for doing things like sneaking whiskey to the soldiers at Fort Howard. And when he "got his Ebenezer up," or got mad, everyone around knew to look out.

Despite his temper, Ebenezer did some good things. He helped build the first road along the Fox River between Green Bay and the Grand Kaukaulin. He served in Wisconsin's very first **territorial legislature**. Ebenezer also built a sawmill for the Stockbridge Indians at Statesburg.

Ebenezer Childs

territorial legislature (**lej** uhs lay chur): a group of people elected by citizens who have the power to make the laws for a territory

And he married the daughter of Augustin Grignon, an important fur trader whose house was right across the river from Statesburg. So whether or not Ebenezer actually asked Electa to marry him, it's quite likely that they knew each other.

Electa did not marry Ebenezer Childs. But soon, an Indian husband came along.

5

Among the Oneida

For a couple of years, from 1830 to 1832, we're not sure what Electa was up to. Puzzle pieces, again, are missing. She might have continued teaching in Statesburg.

We do know that on Monday, September 17, 1832, she started teaching at a school in Smithfield, Wisconsin.

Smithfield, another Indian village on the Fox River, was not far from Statesburg. Today, it is part of the village of Kimberly. Electa's new school had about 30 students.

A few months earlier, a young **Methodist** missionary had come to Smithfield. His name was Daniel Adams. Daniel was a Mohawk Indian from Canada.

Before he moved to Wisconsin, Daniel worked as a missionary to the Oneida Indians in New York.

Methodist: a Christian group known especially for sending out missionaries

Daniel was good at his job. In New York, he convinced 100 Oneida Indians to join his church.

Daniel could speak the Oneida language, and many other Indian languages, too. He was tall like Electa, and he was handsome. Thomas Morris, a Methodist **bishop**, called him an "excellent man." And he was a good singer.

On Sunday, September 16, the day before Electa's school opened, Daniel and **Reverend** John Clark, a minister from New York City, held a church service at Smithfield. The service took place in a newly built mission house made of logs. Once again, the mission house also served as Electa's school.

Electa's schools in Statesburg and Smithfield probably looked similar to this one.

bishop: a high-ranking church leader   **reverend**: the title for a pastor or minister

Soon, John Clark moved on to visit other churches. He left Daniel in charge of the church at Smithfield and Electa in charge of the school.

"We have so many good meetings here," Daniel wrote in 1832 in a letter to John Clark. "I have, indeed, for my part, experienced the greatest blessings."

Daniel had another reason to be happy. He and Electa would soon be married. Their wedding was on July 25, 1833, in Statesburg. John Clark was the minister. He was a close friend. Electa and Daniel later named one of their sons, John Clark Adams, after him.

In 1833, John Clark wrote that Electa's students were doing well in every subject. They were especially good in geography, math, and history.

Electa and Daniel didn't live in Smithfield very long. The village was on land owned by the Menominee Indians.

In a **treaty** in 1822, the Menominee had agreed to let the Stockbridge and Oneida Indians live on their land along the Fox River.

The Indians from New York thought that they had bought the land. But the Menominee believed that they were only sharing the land with the New York tribes.

In 1831 and 1832, 2 new treaties ended the disagreement. The

WHI IMAGE ID 4791

Menominee chief Ma-ko-me-ta in 1827. Long before the Stockbridge Indians came to Wisconsin, other Indian tribes lived there.

Menominee **ceded** millions of acres to the United States government, including the land that contained Statesburg and Smithfield. The Stockbridge Indians agreed to leave Statesburg and to move to Calumet County on the eastern shore of Lake Winnebago. The Oneida Indians said they would move to

treaty: an official written agreement between countries or peoples   **ceded** (**seed** ed): gave up

Duck Creek, near Green Bay. Some Oneida Indians were already living there. Today, the Oneida Nation of Wisconsin still has a reservation along the creek.

Electa and Daniel went to live at Duck Creek, too. There they lived in a house made of logs. Once again, Daniel worked in the church and Electa taught school.

Daniel and Electa lived at Duck Creek until 1836. Then, changes came to Wisconsin.

In 1836, Wisconsin became its own US territory. Wisconsin Territory was big. It included all of what would later be the states of Wisconsin, Iowa, and Minnesota, as well as parts of North and South Dakota. Wisconsin was no longer a part of Michigan Territory. Michigan was getting ready to become a state in 1837.

Soon, Wisconsin Territory began to look a lot like New York had before the Stockbridge Indians left. Lots of white settlers began moving in. The Menominee and other Indian tribes continued to cede land to the US government.

A map of Wisconsin Territory in 1836

As in New York, the Indian land was resold to white settlers to build their homes and farms and to companies that built roads and cities.

Also around this time, the US government created a place called Indian Territory. Indian Territory was far away from

Wisconsin, but lots of Indians were living there. Daniel knew many of the languages spoken there. He wanted to go there to teach Indians to be Christians.

Daniel and Electa had a big decision to make. Should they stay in Wisconsin? Or should they move to Indian Territory, where Daniel could work as a missionary?

The Great Seal of the Territory of Wisconsin

6
Indian Territory

In 1836, Daniel and Electa decided to move to Indian Territory. That year, Daniel visited a church in Illinois. He sang and spoke in the Mohawk language. People at the church gave him $193 to buy a horse and to pay for their move.

The United States government had created Indian Territory in 1834. It was a big place. What was once Indian Territory is today the states of Oklahoma, Kansas, Nebraska, and part of Iowa.

Most Indians did not get to choose whether to live in Indian Territory. The **Indian Removal Act** forced most Indians who lived east of the Mississippi River to leave their homes and move there. By 1840, more than 60,000 native people were living in Indian Territory.

Indian Removal Act: a law passed in 1830 that required all Native Americans living in the southern United States to move west of the Mississippi River

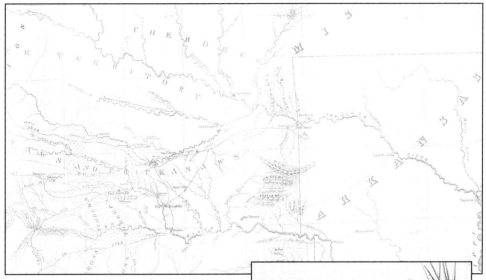

A map of part of Indian Territory, showing the area where Electa and Daniel lived

In the 1830s and 1840s, Indians were forced to move west of the Mississippi River.

Some Indians in the territory were very poor. They lived in tents made from animal skins or tiny huts made from wood and mud. The poorest Indians did not have farms. They relied on food sent by the US government. Many were sick.

A town in Indian Territory

However, other Indians were doing well. They lived in 2-story houses on large, fenced-in farms with crops, cows, and horses. They wore nice clothes. Some owned African American slaves. Major General Ethan Allen Hitchcock of the US Army, who visited Indian Territory from 1841 to 1842, said one Cherokee Indian's home had carpet on the floor, lots of **mahogany** furniture, and a beautiful piano.

General Hitchcock said some Indians lived in traditional ways. They wore Indian blankets and clothes with feathers,

mahogany (muh **hog** uh nee): a hard, dark, and reddish brown wood from a tropical tree

WHI IMAGE ID 23639

Many Indians played a ball-and-stick game similar to today's game of lacrosse.

spoke their native languages, and held traditional Indian ceremonies and dances. In his diary, Hitchcock wrote about watching a traditional Indian game played with balls and sticks.

Others in Indian Territory spoke and wrote English well, went to church, and had given up many traditional Indian ways of living. General Hitchcock went to a fancy Cherokee ball where women wore beautiful gowns and the guests danced to fiddle music.

Daniel and Electa lived a couple of miles outside of Indian Territory, near what today is Seneca, Missouri. The name of the town comes from one of the tribes in Indian Territory. The Seneca Indians were from New York. Daniel's job as a missionary was to teach them about the Christian religion.

At first, Daniel and Electa were excited to live near Indian Territory. Their first son, Alex, was born soon after they arrived, and they were happy. But then life became harder.

Teaching the Seneca Indians about Christianity had seemed like a good job for Daniel. He could speak the Seneca language. But even though the Seneca Indians liked Daniel, they weren't interested in becoming Christians.

After nearly 2 years of trying, Daniel still had not convinced one Seneca Indian to join his church. "He has had no success," wrote Reverend Jacob Lanius, who visited Daniel and Electa in 1839. Daniel was discouraged. "Sometimes he has a little **congregation**, others none at all. The **prospect** is dark, very dark," Lanius wrote.

congregation: a group of people who gather for a religious service   **prospect**: a possibility for the future

58

But Daniel and Electa still had many reasons to be happy. They lived in "a neat little cabin, better than many in the state . . . with 2 beds, a table, trunks . . . and the best library I have seen in the district, **save** one," Lanius said.

Daniel had started farming, and he seemed good at it. The land in Indian Territory was mostly flat plains, which was good for farming. Daniel grew wheat and corn.

Electa was smart, Jacob Lanius wrote. He called her "one of the most intelligent ladies I have seen for days . . . many days. She has a good mind and a very good English education."

Like this farmer, Daniel grew wheat.

save: except for

And Lanius said they had a son, Alex. They were planning to teach him "in English first and afterward in Indian."

"I enjoyed myself well with this family," he wrote.

Soon, 2 more sons arrived. Daniel Jr. was born in 1840 and John Clark in 1842.

In 1842, 2 Quaker visitors stayed at Daniel and Electa's house. They talked about many things with Electa, including the Quaker school that she had gone to in New York as a girl.

After traveling through Indian Territory and meeting many Indians, the visitors were surprised that Electa and Daniel's 3 sons were dressed like white children and spoke English. Most Indians they had met were more traditional. The visitors said the family lived in a new house made of boards, not logs. They were impressed with Electa. "Her whole conduct and conversation were dignified," the visitors wrote.

Electa was smart, they said. She talked easily about complicated subjects such as Indian treaties. Daniel and

Electa told their guests that many Indians didn't like white people because of the way white people treated them. And the visitors noted that Daniel still had not found any Seneca Indians interested in joining his church.

Soon after this visit, Electa's life took a terrible turn. On March 3, 1844, Daniel died. We don't know how he died, but Electa was left to raise 3 young boys on her own.

A few weeks later, another church leader visited Electa. She was all alone, the visitor wrote. There was no one nearby who shared her Christian beliefs. "She is **abundantly** qualified, and would doubtless **devote** herself, if encouragement were extended, to the care of a female school," he wrote. But there was no school nearby where Electa could teach.

abundantly (uh **buhn** duhnt lee): more than enough   **devote**: give time, energy, and attention

7

Among the Cherokee

A few months after Daniel died, a memorable event occurred at Electa's house. A group of church leaders from across the United States visited. They were headed to an important meeting near **Tahlequah**, Oklahoma. At this meeting, they were going to discuss sending missionaries into a huge area of land that stretched to the west of Indian Territory. The missionaries would teach the Indians there about Christianity.

A few days before the meeting, 60 people filled Electa's house for a church service. It was Sunday, October 20, 1844. There were Indians, African Americans, and white people. Many of them were traveling to the meeting in Tahlequah.

One of Electa's guests was Bishop Thomas Morris. Later, Bishop Morris wrote about the visit in his diary. He said

Tahlequah: tah **lee** kwah

IMAGE COURTESY OF THE UNITED METHODIST NEWS SERVICE

Missionaries often had to travel long distances to faraway places.

Electa was smart and well educated. He said being a Christian was important to her.

Although he didn't mention such a conversation in his diary, it's possible that Bishop Morris and Electa talked about **slavery**. It was an important topic of conversation at the time. Owning African American slaves was legal then in the United States. Disagreement over slavery would eventually lead to the Civil War in 1861. Already in 1844, many people thought that slavery should end.

slavery: the practice of owning people and making them work

In May 1844, a few months before Bishop Morris visited Electa, the leaders of his church, known as the Methodist **Episcopal** Church, had argued about slavery. Church leaders who lived in the northern part of the United States said slavery was wrong. Church leaders who lived in the southern United States said that it was all right to own slaves. The southerners got angry. They voted to **secede** from the northern church. They created their own church, the Methodist Episcopal Church South.

Bishop Thomas Morris believed that slavery was wrong. He stayed with the northern church. For nearly 100 years after this, there were separate northern and southern Methodist Episcopal churches.

LIBRARY OF CONGRESS, PRINTS AND PHOTOGRAPHS DIVISION, LC-DIG-CWPBH-03476

Bishop Thomas Morris

Episcopal: i **pis** kuh puhl   **secede** (si **seed**): to leave or withdraw from a group or an organization, often to form another

Many Cherokee Indians were at the meeting in Tahlequah, too. Tahlequah was the capitol of the Cherokee Nation in Indian Territory. Soon, the Cherokee Nation would become very important to Electa.

On Christmas Day in 1845, Electa married a Cherokee Indian named John Walker Candy. Their wedding was near Seneca, Missouri, where Electa had lived with Daniel Adams.

John was born in Tennessee around 1806. Like Electa, he went to boarding school. He had also been married once before. He had 4 daughters. His first wife, Mary Ann Watie, had died in 1844.

Mary Ann came from a very important Cherokee family. Her brother, Elias Boudinot, was the **editor** of the *Cherokee Phoenix* newspaper. It was the very first Indian newspaper in the US. The *Cherokee Phoenix* was **bilingual**, printed in both English and Cherokee. It was first published in Georgia in 1828. John Walker Candy had worked at the *Cherokee Phoenix* as a **printer**.

editor: a person who decides what should go in a newspaper, magazine, or book **bilingual** (bɪ **ling** gwuhl): spoken or written in 2 different languages **printer**: a person whose job or business is printing text or images on paper

The front page of the *Cherokee Phoenix*. The newspaper was printed in both Cherokee and English.

Mary Ann's family played a big role in bringing the Cherokees to Indian Territory. In 1835, her brother Elias, cousin John Ridge, and uncle Major Ridge signed a treaty. The treaty said that the Cherokee Indians would move from Georgia to Indian Territory. Other Cherokee Indians signed the treaty, too.

However, most of the tribe did not want to leave Georgia. The treaty made them angry. But once it was signed, they had to go. In the winter of 1838-1839, the Cherokee set out for Indian Territory. Their new home was far away and the winter was harsh. Thousands of Cherokee Indians died while walking to Indian Territory. Their journey became known as the Cherokee Trail of Tears.

After they arrived in Indian Territory, many Cherokee remained angry about the treaty. They wanted revenge. They set out to kill those who had signed the treaty in 1835. In 1839, Mary Ann's brother, cousin, and uncle were killed. Many others who had signed the treaty were killed, too.

Meanwhile, John kept busy working as a printer. In Indian Territory, he worked for a second newspaper, the *Cherokee Advocate*. He also printed sections of the Bible that were translated into Cherokee, as well as Cherokee **almanacs**, hymn books, school books, and Bible story books. He even printed books in other Indian languages, such as **Choctaw** and **Muskogee**. One of his biggest projects, in 1842, was printing 1,000 copies of the **constitution** and laws of the Cherokee Nation.

almanac: a book published once a year with facts on many subjects **Choctaw**: chok taw
Muskogee: muh **skoh** gee **constitution**: the formal written laws and plans of government

A Cherokee Printer

When John Walker Candy was working as a printer, the job was much tougher than today. There were no computers in the 1800s.

To form a word, a printer picked tiny metal letters out of a wooden box. The letters, called type, were made of lead. Lining them up to create words was called **composing** type. Once the words were composed, they were coated in ink and pressed onto paper to make a printed page. The whole process was done on a machine called a printing press. There was no electricity. Printing presses were powered by steam engines or operated by hand.

RESEARCH DIVISION OF THE OKLAHOMA HISTORICAL SOCIETY

Printers working on the Cherokee Advocate

composing: putting something together

John's job was even tougher because the *Cherokee Phoenix* and the *Cherokee Advocate* were printed in both English and Cherokee. Often, articles that appeared in the newspaper first had to be translated from English into Cherokee. John helped with the translating.

Reading in their own language was something new for the Cherokee. An alphabet, with 86 letters, was created in the 1820s by a Cherokee Indian named Sequoyah. Before this, the Cherokee had a spoken language but no written one.

Once they had a written language, the Cherokee Indians were able to start a newspaper and print books and other things. Having printed words kept them informed. For the first time, the Cherokee were able to publish their views on important topics, such as the Trail of Tears.

For a few years after John and Electa were married, what we know about her life comes entirely from what we know about him. Electa doesn't seem to have worked as a teacher. She was probably busy raising her 3 sons and 4 stepdaughters. We know that John and Electa spent some of this time in Arkansas, just outside of Indian Territory.

They may also have lived in Missouri and in Indian Territory, where John worked as a printer. And for a little while, they lived in Texas.

In 1846, the Cherokee Indians were still fighting among themselves. "I think there is now to be no end to bloodshed," John wrote to Mary Ann's brother Stand Watie on April 10 of that year. The families of those who had signed the 1835 treaty, forcing the Cherokee to move to Indian Territory, were still in danger. This included John, Electa, and their 7 children.

John and Electa decided that Indian Territory was not a safe place for their family. They would to move to Texas. There the family would be safe. They were not alone. Other Cherokee families fled to Texas, too.

In Texas, there was sadness. John's youngest daughter, 7-year-old Sarah Jane, died there in 1846.

A new treaty signed in 1846 settled the fighting among the different groups of Cherokee. Soon after this, John and Electa returned to Indian Territory.

In 1847, John was back working as a printer. He worked in Tahlequah and in what today is Park Hill, Oklahoma. In 1852, he was elected to Tahlequah's first town council.

Then, once again, Electa's life changed.

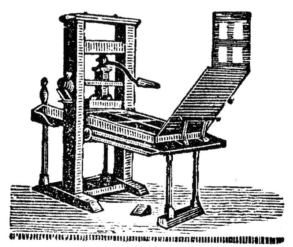

A printing press

8

Return to Wisconsin

In 1855, Electa had a big decision to make. Back in Wisconsin, Electa's brother John W. Quinney was sick. He knew he would die soon. He wanted Electa to come back and see him.

Electa had been living in Indian Territory for nearly 20 years. Her sons, who were now teenagers, had grown up there. John Walker Candy's family was there, too, and he had a good job as a printer. What should she do?

Electa traveled to Wisconsin. Her husband and sons came along. She was with her brother when he died on July 21, 1855, at his farm in the town of Stockbridge, near Lake Winnebago.

While Electa was away, Wisconsin had changed. It became a state in 1848. There were now railroads, cities, and many

WHI IMAGE ID 6554

More people lived in Wisconsin when Electa returned in 1855. Milwaukee was becoming a city.

more people. When her brother John died, he left Electa his farm. This gave her a place to live in Wisconsin. She decided to stay. She did not go back to Indian Territory.

Her farm sat along what was then called the Military Road. Margaret Daun, whose family lived there many years after Electa, said the house was originally a log cabin. Later, the logs were covered with boards. The house had 2 bedrooms upstairs and a kitchen, living room, and bedroom downstairs. There was also a barn, a shed, and some other small buildings. The farm sat on a hill overlooking Lake Winnebago. The lake was about a mile away.

The Military Road

Electa's farm was near the village of Stockbridge alongside the Military Road. This was the first real road in Wisconsin. Work on the Military Road began in 1835. Some stretches followed old Indian trails.

The Military Road had an important purpose. It was built to connect the state's 3 military forts: Fort Crawford, Fort Winnebago, and Fort Howard. Once it was built, settlers could get around more easily. They could travel from Green Bay all the way to Prairie du Chien. As a result, many people began moving to Wisconsin. Today, what was once the Military Road through Stockbridge is part of State Highway 55.

COURTESY OF THE AUTHOR

The Military Road

But life back in Wisconsin was hard. John Walker Candy had hoped to start a newspaper for the Stockbridge Indians. He never did. He had a very hard time finding any job. "Instead of supporting his wife he was supported by her," a friend later said.

John wasn't the only person struggling to find work. In 1857, the entire United States suffered a sudden, terrible **financial panic**. It continued until 1859. Many people lost their jobs. Many banks and businesses failed. The panic was worst near the Great Lakes, including in the state of Wisconsin.

In 1857, the entire United States suffered a sudden financial panic.

LIBRARY OF CONGRESS, PRINTS AND PHOTOGRAPHS DIVISION, LC-USZ6-952

financial panic: a sudden, widespread fear about money

A Panic and a Painting

Just how difficult was the Panic of 1857? We find a clue in the story of a portrait of Electa's brother John W. Quinney.

The portrait was painted in 1849. In July 1857, after John had died, Electa agreed to give it to the Wisconsin Historical Society. John had been an important Stockbridge leader, and the historical society would be able to **preserve** his portrait. Electa sent it to Fond du Lac to be framed. Then the panic hit.

The portrait of John W. Quinney

In January 1858, the portrait was still at the frame shop in Fond du Lac. Electa owed $8.50 for the framing and could not pay the bill. The shop owner refused to send the painting to the historical society until he was paid.

Electa apologized in a letter to Lyman Draper, the secretary of the historical society. "Owing to disappointments and **adverse** fortune . . . I have not been able to **redeem** [the portrait] in

preserve: carefully save for the future   adverse: bad or negative   redeem: to pay off a debt so that an item is yours order to send it to you," Electa wrote. "Be patient. . . . I will redeem it and have it sent on as soon as circumstances will permit."

Eventually, a man who was working with the historical society paid the bill for Electa. Today, the Wisconsin Historical Society still owns the painting.

In 1859, John returned to Indian Territory, while Electa stayed in Wisconsin. We don't know why he left. This is one more missing puzzle piece in Electa's life. Maybe he thought he would have better luck finding a job in Indian Territory. We also don't know why Electa stayed behind, but perhaps she had to stay to look after her farm. John's daughter Elizabeth, who had been visiting Wisconsin, left with him. Electa's family and friends were surprised.

"You say that Mr. Candy and [his] daughter . . . will leave soon but you do not inform us of the place of their destination. Are they going to Keshena, Kansas gold mines, Cherokee nation or where?" Electa's friend Levi Konkapot Jr. asked in a letter in February 1859.

"Where is Uncle Candy?" Electa's nephew Jeremiah Slingerland wrote in July 1859. "I heard he and Elizabeth were at Portage. Is it so? Foolish things, what are they doing? Don't they want to return?"

Around the time that John left, Electa lived for a little while on the Stockbridge-Munsee reservation in Shawano County. The reservation was about 80 miles north of her farm in Stockbridge. She had a house and a garden on the reservation. Her sons sometimes traveled north to the reservation, too. They were growing up. In 1859, Alex was 21, Daniel was 19, and John was 17 years old.

"Daniel has been up here," Jeremiah Slingerland wrote that year. "I don't know what he came after but to steal some of our girls," Jeremiah joked.

But by 1860, Electa had moved back to Stockbridge. Electa's friends tried to get her to return to the reservation.

"I passed your place the other day, your little garden spot looks well," one friend wrote in 1860. "I often think how pleasant it would be if you were living here."

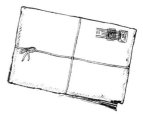

Jeremiah's wife, Sarah, thought so too. "If you were . . . living up here I should feel that . . . I had a dear friend near me," Sarah wrote in 1862.

Back in Stockbridge, Electa was very poor. Her sons tried to help. But their farm was small. She could not grow enough food to feed her family. "I am really very sorry that you have yet so much hardship, so many to feed . . . it is very discouraging to be so burdened," Sarah wrote in 1860.

Between 1859 and 1863, John Walker Candy wrote 2 letters to Electa. We don't know what he wrote or the dates that the letters were written. But we do know a little bit about what happened to him in those years.

John was living in Arkansas, just outside of Indian Territory. He doesn't seem to have been working as a printer. His name doesn't appear on anything printed in Indian Territory after 1855.

Indian Territory was a terrible place to live at this time. During the Civil War, which began in 1861, there were many battles in and near Indian Territory. One famous battle, in Maysville, Arkansas, in October 1862, was near John's home. Mary Ann Watie's brother, Stand, was a Confederate general, and he led troops in this battle.

Throughout the Civil War, the Cherokee Indians disagreed over whether to support the **Union** or the **Confederacy**. We don't know which side John agreed with. But we do know that the Civil War years were hard for him in Indian Territory.

LIBRARY OF CONGRESS, PRINTS AND PHOTOGRAPHS DIVISION, LC-USZ6-952

The Civil War was a difficult time in Indian Territory.

Union: the group of states that remained loyal to the US government during the Civil War; the North
Confederacy: the group of 11 Southern states that fought against the Union during the Civil War; the South

Two of his daughters, Susan and Elizabeth, died within a few weeks of each other in 1862. In 1863, John's son-in-law died of **pneumonia** while fighting in the war. And several of his grandchildren died in the 1860s.

In Wisconsin, Electa was having a hard time, too. On October 16, 1861, her son Daniel signed up to fight for the Union. The next year he left for Missouri with the Second Wisconsin Volunteer **Cavalry**.

A soldier from the Second Wisconsin Volunteer Cavalry

The Second Wisconsin Volunteer Cavalry in St. Louis, Missouri

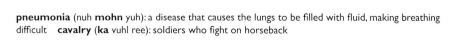

pneumonia (nuh **mohn** yuh): a disease that causes the lungs to be filled with fluid, making breathing difficult   **cavalry** (**ka** vuhl ree): soldiers who fight on horseback

81

Daniel believed in what he was doing. "I will try and come home when peace is declared, if health and life is spared, and not before," he wrote to Electa in August 1862.

Daniel wrote many letters to Electa. Some of the letters were funny. Once, Daniel joked about a photo that had been taken of him in which he didn't look very handsome. Another time, he wrote about some Stockbridge-Munsee tribal leaders who he said were not very well educated. They were running in a tribal election, hoping to become chief. "I believe in a chief knowing how to read and write, don't you think so too?" he asked Electa.

Daniel often asked Electa about her farm and their friends in Wisconsin. He also sent Electa some of his pay. He worried that it wasn't enough. "If you

Many Native Americans from Wisconsin signed up to fight in the Civil War, including these 2 Stockbridge.

82

LIBRARY OF CONGRESS, PRINTS AND PHOTOGRAPHS DIVISION, LC-DIG-PPMSCA-33755

A Civil War military hospital

are in need of more money just tell me and I will send you all that I [have] got," Daniel wrote in August 1862.

Daniel also said in this letter that he was sick. "I don't feel very well. There are a great many of our boys getting sick," he wrote. "I don't think that the hospital doctors know any too much. . . . All that he gave me was powders, powders. Do you know what would be good [to take]?"

"I wish you all were down here," he added.

But Daniel would not see his family again. On February 21, 1863, he died of pneumonia. He was buried in Springfield, Missouri. Around this time, Electa's son Alex also died. Alex was buried in the town of Stockbridge.

These were, indeed, sad years for Electa.

In 1862, her niece Sarah went through a tough time. Someone in Sarah's family had died. She thanked Electa for thinking about her troubles "when you have a wounded heart of your own to bear. I deeply feel for you," she wrote.

9
Still a Teacher

After the Civil War, Electa's life did not get easier. But she had lots of close friends and her remaining family. They helped her get through. She took care of them, too.

Because her son had died in the war, Electa received 8 dollars each month from the US government. Some of that money fed people Electa let stay at her farm.

Electa's nephew Jeremiah wasn't happy that she was taking care of others when she barely had enough money for herself. "I am sorry that you give him shelter, [and that you] work yourself to death," he wrote about one guest in 1867. But Electa wanted to do what she could for others.

What we know about the last years of Electa's life comes mostly from letters that other people wrote to her.

WHI IMAGE ID 66883

The eastern shore of Lake Winnebago, near where Electa lived

Electa's family and friends wrote about lots of different things, such as the weather, farm crops, visitors to their homes, and tribal **politics**. But we only have one side of the conversation. Unfortunately, none of Electa's letters back were saved.

In 1870, Electa's nephew Benjamin thanked Electa for letting him stay at her house after his mother died. "I will never forget the kindness I received from you when I was there," he wrote. The feeling "was the same as when my mother was alive."

politics: having to do with government or the work of government leaders

86

One letter reveals that Electa's son John thought of becoming a teacher like his mother. "You tell John Clark to come out here and teach when he gets ready to do so," wrote a friend from Iowa.

Being a Christian was still important to Electa. Friends often mentioned passages from the Bible. Sarah once answered difficult Bible quiz questions that Electa had sent to her.

"What king gave to another king 20 cities and he was not pleased with the gift and what did he say? You will find the answer in the 11th, 12th and 13th verses of the 9th chapter of 1st Kings," Sarah wrote. "I will try to answer the other questions as soon as I can."

Religion was important to many Stockbridge, including Electa. This special Bible was given to the tribe in 1745 and now sits in their museum.

Although John Walker Candy never returned to Wisconsin, letters help us know what was going on in his life. Some letters that mention John were written to Electa by her friends. Others were between people who knew John in Arkansas.

John was apparently angry about things that had divided the Cherokee people for many years. In 1867, he tried to get a **pamphlet** printed about his views, but he could not interest anyone in the project.

In 1867, John's nephew William Boudinot wrote a strange letter about him to Stand Watie.

"Jack Candy has gone crazy and appeared to me this morning. I am sorry to say this is no joke. He is really out of his wits," William wrote.

We don't know what went on that day, but John died in Arkansas about a year later, on August 21, 1868. On the day he died, he had walked 8 miles to church and back.

pamphlet: a small booklet that usually contains information on a single topic

WHI IMAGE ID 97958

A lot of what we know about Electa comes from letters. Her son Daniel Adams wrote this one to her in 1862, a few months before he died of pneumonia.

His former brother-in law, John Wheeler, wrote that he had been "an honest, upright, good man." John Wheeler's wife and Mary Ann Watie were sisters. Like John Walker Candy, he worked as a printer.

Electa heard the news and shared it. Others wrote back, sharing her sadness.

"I am sorry to hear that Mr. Candy has gone to his long home," wrote Electa's friend Marion Peters. "I hope he has gone to a better world than this."

Finally, in these years, those who knew Electa still saw her as a teacher. They seemed to know that Electa, like any teacher, would be unhappy if she found errors in their letters to her.

"I hope you will overlook all my mistakes. I write this very fast," her nephew Benjamin wrote in 1870.

"You will please look over all my mistakes," Marion Peters wrote in 1870.

Years later, after Electa had died, a woman from Stockbridge said neighbors always thought of her as a teacher. "My father's father, I think, knew her," the woman said. She remembered that her father always said "the schoolteacher" when talking about Electa.

10

A Tribal Fight

Many Stockbridge Indians, including Electa's son Daniel, fought in the Civil War. But it was not their only fight in the 1860s.

There was also a big tribal fight going on. Just like the North and South in the Civil War, the Stockbridge-Munsee tribe became divided into 2 sides. But instead of guns and cannons, this battle was fought on paper and with words. Instead of generals, it was led by lawyers.

This fight went on for 50 years. It began in the 1840s, while Electa was living in Indian Territory, and ended in the 1890s, a few years after she died.

What did they fight about for so long? The Stockbridge-Munsee Indians disagreed on a question that was very important to the future of their tribe. Should they all remain members of the Stockbridge-Munsee tribe? Or should some of them leave the tribe and become citizens of the United States?

There would be consequences for those who left. They would no longer be allowed to live on the Stockbridge-Munsee reservation. They would no longer be allowed to vote in tribal elections. And those who left would no longer get a share of money paid to the tribe, as happened sometimes, such as when land on the reservation was sold. Were they willing to give all of that up?

But Stockbridge-Munsee men who became US citizens would be able to help choose the US president and vote in other important US elections. At the time, women could not vote in US elections. And living off the reservation might not be so bad, some Stockbridge-Munsee thought. On the reservation, land could only be sold with approval from the US government. But if they became US citizens and owned land off the reservation, they could sell that land whenever they wanted, without having to ask permission.

Those who wanted to remain in the tribe called themselves the Indian Party. Those who wanted to become US citizens called themselves the Citizens Party.

What the Indian and Citizens Parties disagreed about, really, was whether to live more like white people.

This was not a new question. Back in 1734, when John Sergeant visited the Mohican Indians in Massachusetts, the tribe had struggled with the same worry. Some Mohicans had disagreed then about letting John Sergeant teach them. They had feared that their Mohican culture would be lost. And as time went by, and the Stockbridge began speaking English instead of Mohican, living in log homes, working on farms, going to church, and dressing in nontraditional clothes, those fears came true. In the 1860s, some Stockbridge Indians said that what remained of their culture would disappear for good if they became US citizens.

Once again, Electa had to make a tough decision. She had to choose one group over the other. Did she agree with the Citizens Party and want to become a US citizen? Or did she agree with the Indian Party and want to stay a member of the tribe?

There was one last thing that complicated her choice. She was a Quinney. And the Quinneys were divided over what to do.

Electa's nephew Jeremiah was a leader in the Indian Party. Many other Quinneys belonged to the Indian Party, so many in fact that it was often called the Quinney Party. But Electa's son John was a leader in the Citizens Party.

Electa had many white friends who were US citizens. She valued what she had learned from white teachers. But her Stockbridge **heritage** was important to her, too. How could she possibly choose one side over the other?

We get one clue to Electa's choice in 1867. That year, her name was on a list of Stockbridge and Munsee Indians who

heritage (**her** uh tij): traditions and culture passed down from generation to generation

Electa's son John Clark Adams

were thinking about leaving the tribe.

But this was just a list of people *thinking* about leaving. The people whose names were on this list remained in the tribe for a few more years.

A more important list came later, in 1871. Electa's name was on this list, too. This time, everyone on the list became US citizens. They were no longer members of the Stockbridge-Munsee tribe.

"Have you been sorry yet that you put your name among those who separate [from the tribe]?" Electa's nephew Jeremiah wrote to her in 1871.

This letter from Jeremiah makes it seem as though Electa made her own choice to become a US citizen in 1871. But did she really put her own name on the list? Some people who were on the 1871 list said later that they hadn't added their names to it. They said their enemies, people who wanted to make their life hard, put their names there. They said it was a way of kicking them out of the Stockbridge-Munsee tribe.

Whether they listed themselves or someone else did it, there were consequences for Stockbridge-Munsee Indians who became US citizens in 1871.

Electa's son John was also on the 1871 list and became a US citizen. At the time, John was studying to be a lawyer at Lawrence University in Appleton. The US government was paying some of his tuition.

In 1872, an Indian Party leader wrote a letter to the US government. He said the government should stop helping John pay his tuition. He said help like that should only be

Lawrence University in 1860

for Indians who belonged to a tribe, not for those who had become US citizens.

In 1873, just a few months before he was going to graduate, John suddenly quit Lawrence University. It's not clear why he quit, but it might be because the US government stopped paying his tuition. In 1874, John tried to go to a different university. The US government said in a letter then that it would not help pay his tuition. John never went back to college. He never earned a college degree.

But even though he was not officially a lawyer, John had learned enough about the law to help others. He especially helped people who said that their names should not have been on the 1871 list.

For the next 20 years, John traveled back and forth to Washington, DC. He asked the US Congress to force the tribe to let these Indians back in.

During these years, while John was often traveling, Electa grew old. On March 7, 1882, she died on her farm in the town of Stockbridge. She was about 75 years old. Electa was buried nearby, in a Stockbridge Indian cemetery.

A few weeks before she died, Electa wrote that she was still of "sound mind, memory and understanding." "Blessed be Almighty God for the same," she wrote.

John inherited her farm. And he continued his fight. Finally, in 1893, John won. The Stockbridge-Munsee had to let those people who wanted to rejoin the tribe back in. A new list was made of those who belonged to the tribe. Those who said they were wrongly put on the 1871 list could be tribal members once again.

But because Electa had died by this time, her name was not on the new list. So we'll never know for sure whether she chose on her own to quit the tribe, or if someone else put her name down. After reading about Electa's life, what do you think happened?

For John, the fight had another terrible consequence. It cost him Electa's farm. His many trips to Washington, DC, were expensive. He ran out of money to pay the taxes and **mortgage** on the farm. In 1889, the bank took the farm away. It was sold at an auction for $286.

John moved to Antigo, Wisconsin. There, on January 27, 1896, he died suddenly after catching a cold.

mortgage (**mor** gij): money lent by a bank to buy a house

11

An Old Trunk

In 1932, nearly 40 years after Electa's son John died, an old wooden trunk that had belonged to him was discovered in a barn near Antigo. Inside was an amazing surprise!

In John's trunk were many things. There was a handwritten list of Stockbridge and Munsee Indians who became US citizens in 1871, including Electa. The truck was stuffed with other papers, too. There were copies of treaties between the United States and the Stockbridge-Munsee tribe and lots of legal papers from the 1800s. Books, letters, a wallet, and a photo of John taken in Washington, DC, in 1876 were there as well.

Incredibly, in all the years that it sat in the barn, the trunk and its contents didn't get wet or damaged. Those who opened it knew right away that it was important. They made sure it was given to people who would preserve it.

John Clark Adams's
trunk

IMAGE COURTESY OF THE STOCKBRIDGE-MUNSEE
COMMUNITY, BAND OF MOHICAN INDIANS

John's trunk became very important to the Stockbridge-Munsee tribe. Inside was information that tribal leaders thought had been lost forever. It helped them understand their history.

There were also many clues to Electa's life. John saved letters that friends and family members wrote to Electa after she returned to Wisconsin in 1855. Some were very special, like the letters that John's brother Daniel wrote to Electa from Missouri before he died in the Civil War.

Thanks to the things that John saved, we know a lot more about Electa's life and a lot more about the Stockbridge Indians. What do these things, and the other puzzle pieces of her life, help us to know about Electa Quinney?

Electa led a remarkable life. She was well educated and comfortable around Indians and white people. She had many friends and was a good mother and an excellent schoolteacher. She talked easily in English about complicated subjects such as Indian treaties. She knew important white and Indian leaders and found herself in situations and places of great importance to Stockbridge, Oneida, and Cherokee Indian history. Because she was there, we understand more about the difficult choices members of these tribes had to make in the 1800s. The story of her life also helps us to know Wisconsin history. Nearly 200 years after she became Wisconsin's first public schoolteacher, Electa is still teaching us today.

Appendix

Electa's Timeline

Around 1807 —   Electa is born in New York.

1814–1822 —   Electa goes to boarding school.

1822–1828 —   Electa teaches school in New York.

1828 —   On June 20, Electa arrives in Wisconsin and begins teaching in Statesburg. This is the first public school in Wisconsin. Electa is the state's first public schoolteacher.

1832 —   On September 17, Electa begins teaching school at Smithfield, Wisconsin.

1833 —   On July 25, Electa marries Daniel Adams. Electa and Daniel move to Duck Creek, Wisconsin.

1836 —   Electa and Daniel move to Missouri.

1838 —   Electa's son Alex is born.

1840 —   Electa's son Daniel is born.

1842 —   Electa's son John is born.

1844 — On March 3, Daniel Adams dies.

On October 20, 60 people, including important church leaders, come to a church service at Electa's house in Missouri.

1845 — On December 25, Electa marries John Walker Candy.

1846 — Electa and John Walker Candy take their family to Texas.

1847 — Electa and John Walker Candy return to Indian Territory.

1855 — Electa, John Walker Candy, and Electa's 3 sons move to the town of Stockbridge, Wisconsin.

On July 21, Electa's brother John W. Quinney dies. He leaves Electa his farm in the town of Stockbridge.

1857 — Electa agrees to give a portrait of her brother John to the Wisconsin Historical Society.

1859 — In February, John Walker Candy returns to Indian Territory.

Electa lives for a little while on the Stockbridge-Munsee reservation near Shawano, Wisconsin.

1860 — Electa moves back to her farm in the town of Stockbridge.

1861 — On October 16, Electa's son Daniel signs up to fight in the Civil War.

1862 — On March 24, Electa's son Daniel leaves for Missouri with the Second Wisconsin Volunteer Cavalry.

1863 — On February 21, Electa's son Daniel dies of pneumonia while fighting in the Civil War. He is buried in Missouri.

1867 — Electa's name is on a list of Stockbridge and Munsee Indians who want to quit the Stockbridge-Munsee tribe to become US citizens.

1868 — On August 21, Electa's second husband, John Walker Candy, dies in Arkansas.

1871 — Electa becomes a US citizen.

1882 — On March 7, Electa dies. She is buried in the town of Stockbridge, Wisconsin.

1896 — On January 27, Electa's son John Clark Adams dies in Antigo, Wisconsin.

1932 — A trunk that had belonged to John Clark Adams is found in Antigo.

Glossary

Pronunciation Key

a	c<u>a</u>t (kat), pl<u>ai</u>d (plad), h<u>a</u>lf (haf)	**oh**	<u>o</u>pen (**oh** puhn), s<u>ew</u> (soh)
ah	f<u>a</u>ther (**fah** THur), h<u>ea</u>rt (hahrt)	**oi**	b<u>oi</u>l (boil), b<u>oy</u> (boi)
air	c<u>a</u>rry (**kair** ee), b<u>ea</u>r (bair), wh<u>ere</u> (whair)	**oo**	p<u>oo</u>l (pool), m<u>o</u>ve (moov), sh<u>oe</u> (shoo)
aw	<u>a</u>ll (awl), l<u>aw</u> (law), b<u>ough</u>t (bawt)	**or**	<u>or</u>der (**or** dur), m<u>ore</u> (mor)
ay	s<u>ay</u> (say), br<u>ea</u>k (brayk), v<u>ei</u>n (vayn)	**ou**	h<u>ou</u>se (hous), n<u>ow</u> (nou)
e	b<u>e</u>t (bet), s<u>ay</u>s (sez), d<u>ea</u>f (def)	**u**	g<u>oo</u>d (gud), sh<u>ou</u>ld (shud)
ee	b<u>ee</u> (bee), t<u>ea</u>m (teem), f<u>ea</u>r (feer)	**uh**	c<u>u</u>p (kuhp), fl<u>oo</u>d (fluhd), butt<u>o</u>n (**buht** uhn)
i	b<u>i</u>t (bit), w<u>o</u>men (**wim** uhn), b<u>ui</u>ld (bild)	**ur**	b<u>ur</u>n (burn), p<u>ear</u>l (purl), b<u>i</u>rd (burd)
ɪ	<u>i</u>ce (ɪs), l<u>ie</u> (lɪ), sk<u>y</u> (skɪ)	**yoo**	<u>u</u>se (yooz), f<u>ew</u> (fyoo), v<u>iew</u> (vyoo)
o	h<u>o</u>t (hot), w<u>a</u>tch (wotch)	**hw**	<u>wh</u>at (hwuht), <u>wh</u>en (hwen)
		TH	<u>th</u>at (THat), brea<u>the</u> (breeTH)
		zh	mea<u>s</u>ure (**mezh** ur), gara<u>g</u>e (guh **razh**)

106

abundantly (uh **buhn** duhnt lee): more than enough

acre (**ay** kur): an area of land almost as large as a football field

adverse: bad or negative

almanac: a book published once a year with facts on many subjects

ancestor: a family member from long ago

assimilated: took in and made as one's own

baptized (**bap** tizd): sprinkled with or dunked in water as a sign of becoming a Christian

bilingual (bi **ling** gwuhl): spoken or written in 2 different languages

bishop: a high-ranking church leader

bluff: a cliff or steep natural wall

boarding school: a school at which students live during the school year

calash: a large, folding hood worn by women in the 1800s

canal: a waterway made by people

catechism (**kat** uh kiz uhm): a manual that teaches religious beliefs

cavalry (**ka** vuhl ree): soldiers who fight on horseback

ceremony (**ser** uh moh nee): a formal event to mark an important occasion

citizen: someone who is an official member of a country or state and has a right to live there

colonial (kuh **loh** nee uhl): of or about a colony

competent (**kom** puh tuhnt): capable

composing: putting something together

Confederacy: the group of 11 Southern states that fought against the Union during the Civil War; the South

congregation: a group of people who gather for religious worship

constitution: the formal written laws and plans of government

culture: the way of life, ideas, and traditions of a group of people

devote: give time, energy, and attention

distinguished (dis **ting** guishd): well known and respected

dormitory: a large room with many beds for sleeping

elevation (eh leh **vay** shun): the height of land

editor: a person who decides what should go in a newspaper, magazine, or book

enchanting: delightful and charming

faithful: loyal and caring

famine: a serious and widespread lack of food

female seminary: a school where girls were taught to be proper ladies

financial panic: a sudden, widespread fear about money

foretold: said ahead of time that some event would happen

fur trade: the exchange of goods such as metal knives and guns for animal pelts

habitat: the place or environment where a plant or animal naturally or normally lives and grows

heartily: deeply and with all your heart

heritage (**her** uh tij): traditions and culture passed down from generation to generation

historian: a person who studies and writes about the past

immigrant (**im** uh gruhnt): someone who leaves one country to permanently live in another country

independence: the right to live freely, without being ruled by another government

Indian agent: someone who worked for the US government and whose job was to communicate with Indian tribes

Indian Removal Act: a law passed in 1830 that required all Native Americans living in the southern United States to move west of the Mississippi River

Indian Territory: a large area of the United States set aside in 1834 where only Indians could live

legal: having to do with laws

lock: a section of a canal that is closed off with gates. A ship can be raised or lowered in a lock by pumping water in or out.

mahogany (muh **hog** uh nee): a hard, dark, and reddish brown wood from a tropical tree

Methodist: a Christian group known especially for sending out missionaries

Michigan Territory: a large area of the northern United States, near the Great Lakes, that included the future states of Michigan, Wisconsin, Iowa, and Minnesota and parts of North and South Dakota

missionary (**mish** uh nair ee): someone who travels to spread a religion and to do good work

mortgage (**mor** gij): money lent by a bank to buy a house

native speaker: a person who learns a language as a baby

orthography (or **thog** ruh fee): spelling

pamphlet: a small booklet that usually contains information on a single topic

persecution: cruel and unfair treatment because of religion or beliefs

pneumonia (nuh **mohn** yuh): a disease that causes the lungs to be filled with fluid, making breathing difficult

politics: having to do with government or the work of government leaders

portaged: carried boats and supplies overland between 2 waterways or around a rough part such as a waterfall

preserve: carefully save for the future

pressured: demanded that someone make a decision

printer: a person whose job or business is printing text or images on paper

prophecy (**prof** uh see): a statement or warning that something will happen in the future

prospect: a possibility for the future

Quaker: a Christian group founded in the 1600s, also called the Religious Society of Friends

rapids: a place in a river where water flows very fast

redeem: to pay off a debt so that an item is yours

remote: far away from other people or cities

reservation: government land reserved or set aside for Indian nations to live on

reverend: the title for a pastor or minister

revolution: a sudden and violent overthrow of a government or ruler

sachem (**sa** chum): tribal leader

save: except for

secede (si **seed**): to leave or withdraw from a group or an organization, often to form another

settlers: people who make their home in a new country or area

slavery: the practice of owning people and making them work

snuffer: a tool used for putting out candles

stenography (stuh **nog** ruh fee): note taking

tax: money paid to a government

temper: a person's usual attitude or mood

territorial legislature (lej uhs lay chur): a group of people elected by citizens who have the power to make the laws for a territory

treaty: an official written agreement between countries or peoples

trespassed: illegally went onto someone else's property

tuition: money paid to take classes

Union: the group of states that remained loyal to the US government during the Civil War; the North

wampum: beads made from polished and carved shells and strung together to make belts, collars, and necklaces

wigwam: a home made of cattail mats or tree bark attached to a framework of small branches

Reading Group Guide and Activities

Discussion Questions

In her life, Electa Quinney had to make many choices. Some were easy and some were very hard to make. What are some easy choices you make every day? Have you ever had to make a hard choice? Describe a time in your life when you were faced with a difficult decision.

Electa mixed Indian and white cultures. What does it mean to mix cultures? In your life, do you mix different cultures? Give an example.

Electa taught in a one-room schoolhouse made of logs. In a one-room schoolhouse, students of all different ages learned together. How is this different from where you go to school? What are some ways that children with different ages might help each other learn?

When Electa was a girl, she went to boarding school. How is boarding school different from schools that you only go to during the day? How might Electa's education have been different if she had gone to a school in her town that had a Stockbridge teacher?

When John Clark Adams's trunk was found in 1932, it was filled with things that he had saved that were important to him. If you were to fill a trunk with the things most important to you, what would go inside? Make a list of the items and explain why you put them in the trunk.

Activities

❧   Wisconsin was a very different place during the time that Electa lived. There were healthier forests, more wild animals, clean rivers and lakes, and much less pollution from mining, industry, and lumbering. Today, many American Indians believe in Seventh Generation practices, a way of thinking about and using our planet's resources that considers the well-being of people who aren't even born yet. Can you think of ways we can work together to preserve our planet for the seventh generation after us? Brainstorm a list with your class and pick your favorites. Then, go out and make it happen!

❧   American Indians have a long and proud history of serving in the United States military, just like Electa's son Daniel, who fought in the Civil War. Do you have people in your family who have served or are serving in the military? Find someone you know and interview them about why they served and what it was like. Ask if you can share what you learned with the class. Do you think American Indians served for similar reasons? Why or why not?

❧   Electa often wrote letters to her friends and family and they wrote back to her. Today, we often send e-mails instead of letters. Try writing a letter on paper to a friend or family member. Get the address from an adult and mail the letter to the person. Ask him or her to write a letter in return and to mail it to you. See how long you can keep up a letter writing exchange through the postal service. How is writing letters different from sending e-mails? Do you find yourself writing about different topics or in different ways?

To Learn More about the Mohican Indians

Bowman, Eva Jean. *Chief Ninham, Forgotten Hero*. Gresham, WI: Muh-he-con-neew Press, 2008.

Davids, Dorothy (adaptor). *Aniishiik: We are Grateful*. Gresham, WI: Muh-he-con-neew Press, 1994.

Heath, Kristina. *Mama's Little One*. Gresham, WI: Muh-he-con-neew Press, 1992.

Loew, Patty. *Native Peoples of Wisconsin*. Madison: Wisconsin Historical Society Press, 2003.

Mohican Indian Facts: http://www.bigorrin.org/mohican_kids.htm.

Weintraub, Aileen, and Shirley Dunn. *The Mohicans*. Fleischmanns, NY: Purple Mountain Press, 2008.

Youth of the Mohican Nation. *The Stories of Our Elders*. Gresham, WI: Muh-he-con-neew Press, 2008.

For Teachers

The Mohican People, Their Lives and Their Lands: A Curriculum Unit for Grades Four–Five. Gresham, WI: Muh-he-con-neew Press, 2008.

Acknowledgments

Many people helped make this book possible. Special thanks to: James Oberly, professor of history at the University of Wisconsin–Eau Claire; Leah Miller and Nathalee Kristiansen at the Arvid E. Miller Memorial Library and Museum in Bowler, Wisconsin; Joe Hermolin at the Langlade County, Wisconsin, Historical Society; the Stockbridge-Munsee Tribal Council and Historical Committee; Jeremy Mohawk of the Stockbridge-Munsee tribe; Margaret Daun of New Holstein, Wisconsin; Jeffrey Siemers; Dorothy Davids and Ruth Gudinas of Muh-he-con-neew Press; Mary Schroeder of the United Methodist Church, Wisconsin Conference, Archives in Sun Prairie, Wisconsin; Loretta Metoxen and Nicolas Reynolds of the Oneida Nation of Wisconsin; Erin Dix at Lawrence University in Appleton, Wisconsin; the Appleton Public Library; Christopher Densmore at the Friends Historical Library in Swarthmore, Pennsylvania; John Finley at the Missouri United Methodist Archives; Dick Williams and Moses Foote at the Clinton, New York, Historical Society; Beverly Mosman and Bill Weige at the Oklahoma Historical Society; Victoria Sheffler at Northeastern State University in Tahlequah, Oklahoma; Christina Wolf at Oklahoma City University; Reverend Homer Noley; Tom Mooney at the Cherokee National Historical Society in Park Hill, Oklahoma; Ann Schillinger at the Cornwall, Connecticut, Historical Society; Robert Dunkelberger, archivist at Bloomsburg University; Deborah Wood at Wilson's Creek National Battlefield in Republic, Missouri; the Norman Rockwell Family Agency; United Methodist News Service; the staff of the Wisconsin Historical Society Library and Archives; Tessa Claire Photography in Deerfield, Wisconsin; the staff of the Wisconsin Historical Society Press, especially Andrew White and Bobbie Malone; the Pierce family, who inspired me to write about a Wisconsin Indian; the Reisner and Kandler families, for my northeast Wisconsin roots; Jennifer Frickelton, who pre-read the manuscript; Eric, Geoff, and Meghan; and Electa, who, I am certain, has been guiding this process every step of the way.

Index

This index points you to the pages where you can read about persons, places, and ideas. If you do not find the word you are looking for, try to think of another word that means about the same thing.

When you see a page number in **bold** it means there is a picture on that page.